The LIFE CYCLE of a PAINTED TURTLE

Andrew Hipp

Photographs by Dwight Kuhn

Rosen Classroom Books & Materials™
New York

For Ken and Sylvia—Andrew Hipp
For Alexis—Dwight Kuhn

Published in 2002 by The Rosen Publishing Group, Inc.
29 East 21st Street, New York, NY 10010

First Edition

Book Design: Michael Caroleo and Michael de Guzman

Project Editor: Emily Raabe

Photo Credits: All photos © Dwight Kuhn.

The author gratefully acknowledges Gary Casper for helpful comments on a draft of this book.

Hipp, Andrew.
The life cycle of a painted turtle / Andrew Hipp.
p. cm. — (The life cycles library)
Includes bibliographical references (p.).
ISBN: 0-8239-5869-8 (lib. bdg.)
ISBN: 1-4042-5207-X (pbk. bdg.)
6-pack ISBN: 1-4042-5208-8
1. Painted turtle—Life cycles—Juvenile literature. [1. Painted turtle. 2. Turtles.] I. Title.
QL666.C547 H57 2002
597.92—dc21 00-013041

Manufactured in the United States of America

Contents

Spring

A painted turtle awakens in February or March. It has been **hibernating**, or sleeping through the winter. Painted turtles hibernate in the mud at the bottom of a pond, in an old muskrat lodge, or hidden on the floor of a forest. After awakening, the painted turtle begins to eat and to search for a **mate**. A male and female prepare for mating by swimming together and touching each other's paws. They then swim to the bottom of the pond to mate.

This turtle has awakened in spring. Some turtles awaken before the ice melts. You might see them swimming beneath the ice.

The Nesting Site

In June or July, female painted turtles look for nesting sites. Turtles must choose their nesting sites very carefully. Turtle eggs are a favorite food of raccoons, snakes, foxes, squirrels, skunks, and crows. Sometimes, almost all the turtle eggs in an area are eaten by these **predators**. The female also must find a site that is not too dry or too wet. If it is too dry, some eggs might not develop. If it is too wet, cool temperatures might slow the babies' **development** and make them hatch out late.

Female turtles travel up to 2,000 feet (610 m) from water to find a nesting site.

Digging the Nest

A painted turtle may take more than 4 hours to dig a nest that is no bigger than your fist. She lays from 4 to 20 eggs in the nest and covers them with soil. Then the mother turtle leaves the nest. She could make as many as five nests before the year is over. She will not return to any of them again. Painted turtles live all across North America, from Canada to Mexico. Painted turtles in the north have a short summer and don't make as many nests as do turtles in the south.

Female turtles dig their nests slowly, kicking the soil away with their feet.

Eggs

Each painted turtle egg is a little bigger than a grape. It is smooth, with a soft, leathery shell that has tiny holes in it. These holes allow an **embryo** inside an egg to breathe. The shell is rich in **calcium**, which the embryo will use to make strong bones. Eggshells are made of several strong layers, but they cannot protect a growing embryo from everything. A flood could drown an embryo. A predator might eat an egg. Plant roots can drill holes right through turtle eggs!

This sandy soil drains well, so when it rains the eggs might not get covered with water.

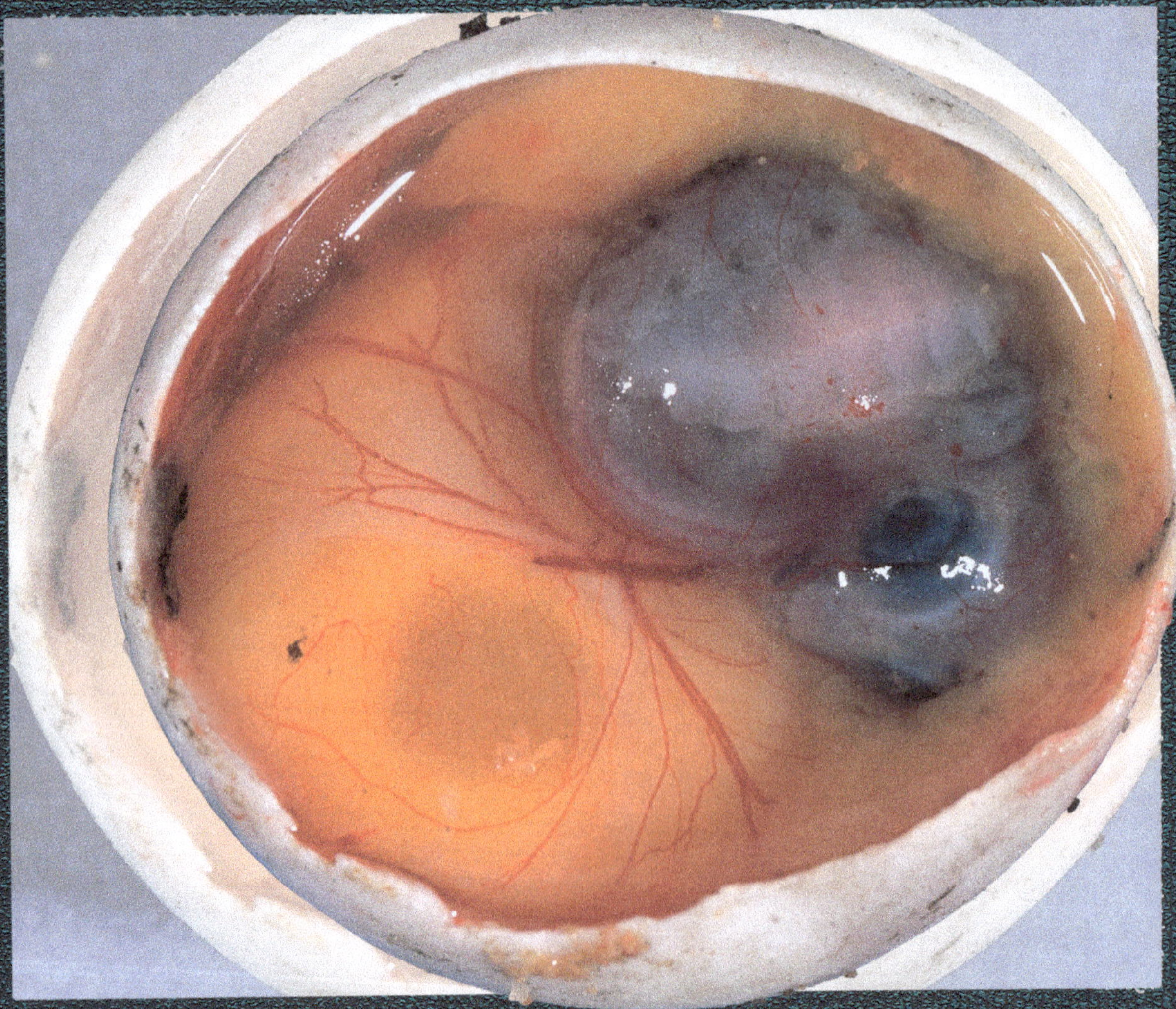

Temperature and Embryos

The weather plays a large role in embryo development. If soil temperature drops below 68 degrees Fahrenheit (20 degrees C) for more than a few weeks, painted turtle embryos might die. Soil temperature also decides what sex the baby turtles will be. Cool nests cause embryos to be males. Warm nests cause embryos to be females. At temperatures that are just right, half of the embryos will be males, and half of them will be females.

Blood vessels run from the embryo to the yolk.

Hatching

After about 72 to 80 days, painted turtle eggs are ready to hatch. Baby turtles use their claws and an **egg tooth** to tear open the soft eggshell. After it hatches, a turtle feeds off the yolk that remains attached to its body. A mother turtle is not around when her babies hatch. Turtle babies must be able to take care of themselves. If the climate where they live is not cold, baby painted turtles might head straight for water. Most of them, though, stay in the nest over winter.

Most baby turtles are about as big around as a quarter.

Winter in the Nest

Baby turtles are able to survive for several weeks in cold weather. However, they might die if the nest temperature drops below 14 degrees Fahrenheit (-10 degrees C). A thick snow on the ground can help keep baby turtles alive. Snow acts like a blanket, keeping the nest warm. In spring or early summer, the turtles climb out of the nest together and head for water. There are no grown turtles to show them where to go. The baby turtles find their way by **instinct**.

These turtles lasted through winter in the nest. Many turtles are not so lucky.

Life in the Water

Ponds provide turtles with food, water, places to hibernate, and places to lie in the sun. Painted turtles eat plants, snails, frogs, insects, and crayfish. As they get older, they eat fewer animals and more plants. Young turtles may be eaten by raccoons, snakes, muskrats, bullfrogs, fish, and even water bugs. Turtles dive underwater or pull their heads into their shells to escape being eaten. Adult turtles have strong shells, but hawks, alligators, eagles, and raccoons still eat them.

The pondweeds in this picture are good food for turtles. They are also a home for the tadpoles, insects, and snails that turtles eat.

Late Summer

Turtles are **reptiles**. Reptiles are **cold-blooded**. This means that their bodies are the same temperature as the air around them. To stay warm, a turtle must lie in the sun, or bask. Painted turtles bask mostly in the morning and in the early afternoon. At night they sleep on the bottom of the pond or marsh, or on a partly sunken log. As days grow shorter and cooler in the fall, the turtles find a place to hibernate. In the spring they will wake up and begin to eat and mate again.

If many turtles are basking in one area, they may push each other. Other times, painted turtles may bask right on top of each other!

Turtles, Turtles Everywhere!

Turtles are an **ancient** group of animals. There were turtles on Earth more than 200 million years ago. Today more than 55 kinds of turtles live in the United States and Canada. Painted turtles are the most common turtle in North America. Look for turtles swimming beneath the ice in early spring or digging nests in early summer. Explore the edge of a pond on a hot afternoon. If you are quiet and look carefully, you might see turtles swimming through the water or basking on a log.

Glossary

ancient (AYN-shent) Very old, having one's beginning long in the past.

calcium (KAL-see-um) A mineral that is an important part of bones, teeth, and eggshells.

cold-blooded (KOLD-BLUD-ed) Having a body temperature that is the same as the environment. Reptiles and amphibians are cold-blooded.

development (dih-VEH-lup-ment) The growth of an organism.

egg tooth (EG TOOTH) A spine at the end of a bird's bill or a turtle's snout, used to break out of the shell in hatching.

embryo (EM-bree-oh) An animal or a plant before it is born, when it is still in the egg, womb, or seed.

hibernating (HY-bur-nayt-ing) Spending the winter in a state of rest.

instinct (IN-stinkt) A way of behaving that a person or an animal is born with and does not have to learn.

mate (MAYT) A partner for making babies. Also, to make babies.

predators (PREH-duh-terz) Animals that kill other animals for food.

reptiles (REP-tylz) Cold-blooded animals that hatch from an egg and have leathery skin, usually covered with scales.

Index

Web Sites

Due to the changing nature of Internet links, PowerKids Press has developed an online list of Web sites related to the subject of this book. This site is updated regularly. Please use this link to access the list: www.powerkidslinks.com/lcl/turtle/